EZ ACCOUNTING

Rita Gritton Mallory

EZACCOUNTING

Rita Gritton Mallory

O'MORE
PUBLISHING

FRANKLIN, TENNESSEE

EZ ACCOUNTING

Copyright © 2008 by Rita Gritton Mallory
ISBN-10   0-9800285-8-2
ISBN-13   978-0-9800285-8-4

Edited by Jessa Rose Sexton
Book design by Paula Rozelle Hanback
Cover concept by Sarah Mallory

Published by:
O'More Publishing
A Division of O'More College of Design
423 South Margin St.
Franklin, TN 37064 U.S.A.

DEDICATION

I am dedicating this book to my two wonderful, loving children, **Sarah Lindsey Mallory and Adam Scot Mallory**. May God fill their lives with the same joy and happiness with which they have filled mine.

INTRODUCTION

Accounting is not a popular conversational topic, but it is a topic that all people will address some time in their lives, whether it be in the form of tax returns, investments, mortgages, loans, checking accounts, or some other financial aspect of their individual life.

Accounting should not be feared; it should be understood. The problem for most people appears to be allowing the fear to overcome the understanding.

I am writing this book at the request of my accounting students in high school and college. I have had numerous students to request a short, quick, easy-to-understand version of the accounting cycle and the terms involved with it.

Due to the requests and the unconditional support of my students, I have attempted to use my expertise to make the information easy to understand and use.

CONTENTS

DEFINITIONS OF KEY TERMS

Assets — anything a business owns

Liabilities — anything a business owes

Equity — the difference between what the business owns and owes

Revenues — income generated in the form of sales revenue or service revenue

Expenses — items that the business uses and must pay for

Accrued Revenues — revenues that have been earned but not yet recorded

Accrued Expenses—expenses that have been incurred but not yet recorded

Contra Account—an account offset against another account

Income Statement—a financial statement listing revenues, expenses, and net income or net loss

Balance Sheet—a financial statement listing assets, liabilities, and equity

Retained Earnings Statement—a summary of the changes in the retained earnings in a company for a specific period of time

THE ACCOUNTING EQUATION

ASSETS = LIABILITIES + EQUITY

ASSETS — LIABILITIES = EQUITY

ASSETS — EQUITY = LIABILITIES

EXAMPLES

Examples of Assets

Cash

Accounts Receivable

Equipment

Supplies

Prepaid Insurance

Examples of Liabilities

Accounts Payable

Notes Payable

Interest Payable

Salaries Payable

Unearned Revenue

Examples of Equity

Capital Accounts

Drawing Accounts

Examples of Revenue

Sales

Business Revenue

Examples of Expenses

Depreciation Expense

Interest Expense

Insurance Expense

Rent Expense

ACCOUNT BALANCES
Increases/Decreases

Assets

Assets carry a debit balance.

Assets are debited when they are increased.

Assets are credited when they are decreased.

Liabilities

Liabilities carry a credit balance.

Liabilities are credited when they are increased.

Liabilities are debited when they are decreased.

Equity

Equity carries a credit balance.

Equity is credited when it is increased.

Equity is debited when it is decreased.

Revenue

Revenues carry a credit balance.

Revenues are credited when they are increased.

Revenue are debited when they are decreased.

Expenses

Expenses carry a debit balance.

Expenses are debited when they are increased.

Expenses are credited when they are decreased.

Dividends

Dividends carry a debit balance.

Dividends are debited when they are increased.

Dividends are credited when they are decreased.

ACCOUNTING CYCLE

The accounting cycle consists of the following steps:

1. Recording entries into the general journal,

2. Posting from the general journal into the general ledger,

3. Preparing a trial balance,

4. Recording adjusting entries into the general journal,

5. Posting the adjusting entries from the general journal into the general ledger,

6. Preparing an adjusted trial balance,

7. Preparing the income statement,

8. Preparing the retained earnings statement,

9. Preparing the balance sheet,

10. Recording the closing entries into the general journal,

11. Posting the closing entries from the general journal to the general ledger, and

12. Preparing a post-closing trial balance.

BUSINESS OPERATION

John Smith opened a printing and office supply business. The following are the accounts and transactions for the month of April 2008.

Accounts and Account Numbers

Cash 101

Accounts Receivable 102

Prepaid Insurance 103

Prepaid Supplies 104

Prepaid Rent. 105

Inventory 106

Equipment 107

Accumulated Depreciation—
Equipment 108

Accounts Payable. 201

1. **Record the following entries in a general journal.**

When recording entries in the general journal these things should be determined:

a. Determine what account(s) are affected.
b. Determine type of account(s) — asset, liability, etc.
c. Determine if account(s) are increased or decreased.
d. Determine which account(s) are debited/credited based on type of account and increase/decrease.

April 1, 2008—John Smith invested $50,000 in the business.

Account › Cash › Asset › Increase › Debit

Account › Equity › Equity › Increase › Credit

April 2, 2008—Supplies were purchased for $500 on account.

Account › Supplies › Asset › Increase › Debit

Account › Accounts Payable › Liability › Increase › Credit

April 3, 2008—Property insurance of $12,000 was paid for 12 months.

Account › Prepaid Insurance › Asset › Increase › Debit

Account › Cash › Decrease › Credit

April 4, 2008—Merchandise worth $5,000 was purchased on account.

Account › Inventory › Asset › Increase › Debit

Account › Accounts Payable › Liability › Decrease › Credit

April 5, 2008—Jones Company purchased $2,000 merchandise on account.

Account › Accounts Receivable › Asset › Increase › Debit

Account › Inventory › Asset › Decrease › Credit

April 6, 2008—Able Company purchased $2,000 merchandise on account.
Account › Accounts Receivable › Asset › Increase › Debit
Account › Inventory › Asset › Decrease › Credit

April 7, 2008—Equipment worth $6,000 was purchased on account (straight-line deprecation for 6 years, no salvage value).
Account › Equipment › Asset › Increase › Debit
Account › Accounts Payable › Liability › Increase › Credit

April 8, 2008—Rent for 12 months ($12,000) was paid.
Account › Prepaid Rent › Asset › Increase › Debit
Account › Cash › Asset › Decrease › Credit

April 9, 2008—Company received $3,000 in revenue from sales.
Account › Cash › Asset › Increase › Debit
Account › Sales › Revenue › Credit

April 10, 2008—Company borrowed $1,000 from bank at 6% for 6 months.
Account › Cash › Asset › Increase › Debit
Account › Notes Payable › Liability › Increase › Credit

General Journal

Date		Description	Post Ref.	Debit	Credit
April	1	Cash	101	50,000	
		John Smith, Equity	301		50,000
	2	Supplies	104	500	
		Accounts Payable	201		500
	3	Prepaid Insurance	103	12,000	
		Cash	101		12,000
	4	Inventory	106	5,000	
		Accounts Payable	201		5,000
	5	Accounts Receivable	102	2,000	
		Inventory	106		2,000
	6	Accounts Receivable	102	2,000	
		Inventory	106		2,000
	7	Equipment	107	6,000	
		Accounts Payable	201		6,000
	8	Prepaid Rent	105	12,000	
		Cash	101		12,000
	9	Cash	101	3,000	
		Sales	401		3,000
	10	Cash	101	1,000	
		Notes Payable	202		1,000

2. Post the entries to a general ledger.

Posting general journal entries to the general ledger is a process of copying each general journal entry to the corresponding account/accounts in the general ledger.

General Ledger

Account: **Cash**   Account No. 101

Date		Item	Post Ref.	Debit	Credit	Balance Debit	Credit
Apr	1		GJ1	50,000		50,000	
	3		GJ1		12,000	38,000	
	8		GJ1		12,000	26,000	
	9		GJ1	3,000		29,000	
	10		GJ1	1,000		30,000	

Account: **Accounts Receivable**   Account No. 102

Date		Item	Post Ref.	Debit	Credit	Balance Debit	Credit
Apr	5		GJ1	2,000		2,000	
	6		GJ1	2,000		4,000	

Account: Prepaid Insurance   **Account No. 103**

Date		Item	Post Ref.	Debit	Credit	Balance Debit	Credit
Apr	3		GJ1	12,000		12,000	

Account: Prepaid Supplies   **Account No. 104**

Date		Item	Post Ref.	Debit	Credit	Balance Debit	Credit
Apr	2		GJ1	500		500	

Account: Prepaid Rent   **Account No. 105**

Date		Item	Post Ref.	Debit	Credit	Balance Debit	Credit
Apr	8		GJ1	12,000		12,000	

Account: Inventory   Account No. 106

Date		Item	Post Ref.	Debit	Credit	Balance	
						Debit	Credit
Apr	4		GJ1	5,000		5,000	
	5		GJ1		2,000	3,000	
	6		GJ1		2,000	1,000	

Account: Equipment   Account No. 107

Date		Item	Post Ref.	Debit	Credit	Balance	
						Debit	Credit
Apr	7		GJ1	6,000		6,000	

Account: Accumulated Depreciation—Equipment   Account No. 108

Date		Item	Post Ref.	Debit	Credit	Balance	
						Debit	Credit

Account: Accounts Payable   **Account No. 201**

Date		Item	Post Ref.	Debit	Credit	Balance	
						Debit	Credit
Apr	2		GJ1		500		500
	4		GJ1		5,000		5,500
	7		GJ1		6,000		11,500

Account: Notes Payable   **Account No. 202**

Date		Item	Post Ref.	Debit	Credit	Balance	
						Debit	Credit
Apr	10		GJ1		1,000		1,000

Account: Interest Payable   **Account No. 203**

Date		Item	Post Ref.	Debit	Credit	Balance	
						Debit	Credit

Account: **John Smith, Capital**　　　　　　**Account No. 301**

Date		Item	Post Ref.	Debit	Credit	Balance Debit	Balance Credit
Apr	1		GJ1		50,000		50,000

Account: **Retained Earnings**　　　　　　**Account No. 302**

Date		Item	Post Ref.	Debit	Credit	Balance Debit	Balance Credit

Account: **Income Summary**　　　　　　**Account No. 303**

Date		Item	Post Ref.	Debit	Credit	Balance Debit	Balance Credit

Account: **Sales**　　　　　　**Account No. 401**

Date		Item	Post Ref.	Debit	Credit	Balance Debit	Balance Credit
Apr	9		GJ1		3,000		3,000

Account: Depreciation Expense   **Account No. 501**

Date		Item	Post Ref.	Debit	Credit	Balance Debit	Balance Credit

Account: Supplies Expense   **Account No. 502**

Date		Item	Post Ref.	Debit	Credit	Balance Debit	Balance Credit

Account: Insurance Expense   **Account No. 503**

Date		Item	Post Ref.	Debit	Credit	Balance Debit	Balance Credit

Account: Rent Expense   **Account No. 504**

Date		Item	Post Ref.	Debit	Credit	Balance Debit	Balance Credit

3. Prepare a trial balance.

Preparation of the trial balance is the process of transferring the balance of each account in the general ledger to the trial balance and calculating debit and credit balances which should equal.

Smith Office Supply
Trial Balance

For Month Ended April 30, 2008

Cash	30,000	
Accounts Receivable	4,000	
Prepaid Insurance	12,000	
Prepaid Supplies	500	
Prepaid Rent	12,000	
Inventory	1,000	
Equipment	6,000	
Accounts Payable		11,500
Notes Payable		1,000
John Smith, Capital		50,000
Sales		3,000
	65,500	65,500

4. Journalize the following adjusting entries.

Value of prepaid rent   ***$11,000***
Account > Rent Expense > expense > increase > debit
Account > Prepaid Rent > asset > decrease > credit

Supplies on hand, April 31   ***$200***
Account > Supplies Expense > expense > increase > debit
Account > Prepaid Supplies > asset > decrease > credit

Value of prepaid insurance   ***$11,000***
Account > Insurance Expense > expense > increase > debit
Account > Prepaid Insurance > asset > decrease > credit

Depreciation on equipment for one month   ***$84***
Equipment value is $6,000 divided by 6 years=
$1,000 per year divided by 12 months=
$84 depreciation for one month
Account > Depreciation Expense > expense > increase > debit
Account > Accumulated Depreciation > Equipment > contra
asset > increase > credit

Interest on note to bank for one month   ***$5***
Bank note was $1,000 at 6% for 6 months=
$1,000 x .06 = $60 divided by 12 months=
$5 x 1 month = $5
Account > Interest Expense > expense > increase > debit
Account > Interest Payable > liability > increase > credit

General Journal

Date		Description	Post Ref.	Debit	Credit
Apr	30	Rent Expense	504	1,000	
		Prepaid Rent	104		1,000
	30	Supplies Expense	502	300	
		Prepaid Supplies	103		300
	30	Insurance Expense	503	1,000	
		Prepaid Insurance	102		1,000
	30	Depreciation Expense	501	84	
		Accumulated Deprecia-tion—Equipment	108		84
	30	Interest Expense	505	5	
		Interest Payable	203		5

5. Post adjusting entries in the general ledger.

Posting adjusting entries into the general ledger is a process of copying the appropriate entry into corresponding account(s) in the general ledger.

General Ledger

Account: Cash   **Account No. 101**

Date		Item	Post Ref.	Debit	Credit	Balance Debit	Balance Credit
Apr	1		GJ1	50,000		50,000	
	3		GJ1		12,000	38,000	
	8		GJ1		12,000	26,000	
	9		GJ1	3,000		29,000	
	10		GJ1	1,000		30,000	

Account: Accounts Receivable   **Account No. 102**

Date		Item	Post Ref.	Debit	Credit	Balance Debit	Balance Credit
Apr	5		GJ1	2,000		2,000	
	6		GJ1	2,000		4,000	

Account: **Prepaid Insurance**   **Account No. 103**

Date		Item	Post Ref.	Debit	Credit	Balance Debit	Balance Credit
Apr	3		GJ1	12,000		12,000	
	30	Adjusting Entry	GJ2		1,000	11,000	

Account: **Prepaid Supplies**   **Account No. 104**

Date		Item	Post Ref.	Debit	Credit	Balance Debit	Balance Credit
Apr	2		GJ1	500		500	
	30	Adjusting Entry	GJ2		300	200	

Account: **Prepaid Rent**   **Account No. 105**

Date		Item	Post Ref.	Debit	Credit	Balance Debit	Balance Credit
Apr	8		GJ1	12,000		12,000	
	30	Adjusting Entry	GJ2		1,000	11,000	

Account: Inventory   **Account No. 106**

Date		Item	Post Ref.	Debit	Credit	Balance Debit	Balance Credit
Apr	4		GJ1	5,000		5,000	
	5		GJ1		2,000	3,000	
	6		GJ1		2,000	1,000	

Account: Equipment   **Account No. 107**

Date		Item	Post Ref.	Debit	Credit	Balance Debit	Balance Credit
Apr	7		GJ1	6,000		6,000	

Account: Accumulated Depreciation—Equipment   **Account No. 108**

Date		Item	Post Ref.	Debit	Credit	Balance Debit	Balance Credit
Apr	30	Adjusting Entry	GJ2		84		84

Account: Accounts Payable   **Account No. 201**

Date		Item	Post Ref.	Debit	Credit	Balance Debit	Credit
Apr	2		GJ1		500		500
	4		GJ1		5,000		5,500
	7		GJ1		6,000		11,500

Account: Notes Payable   **Account No. 202**

Date		Item	Post Ref.	Debit	Credit	Balance Debit	Credit
Apr	10		GJ1		1,000		1,000

Account: Interest Payable   **Account No. 203**

Date		Item	Post Ref.	Debit	Credit	Balance Debit	Credit
Apr	30	Adjusting Entry	GJ2		5		5

Account: John Smith, Capital   Account No. 301

Date		Item	Post Ref.	Debit	Credit	Balance Debit	Balance Credit
Apr	1		GJ1		50,000		50,000

Account: Retained Earnings   Account No. 302

Date		Item	Post Ref.	Debit	Credit	Balance Debit	Balance Credit

Account: Income Summary   Account No. 303

Date		Item	Post Ref.	Debit	Credit	Balance Debit	Balance Credit

Account: Sales   Account No. 401

Date		Item	Post Ref.	Debit	Credit	Balance Debit	Balance Credit
Apr	9		GJ1		3,000		3,000

Account: Depreciation Expense   Account No. 501

Date		Item	Post Ref.	Debit	Credit	Balance	
						Debit	Credit
Apr	30	Adjusting Entry	GJ2	84		84	

Account: Supplies Expense   Account No. 502

Date		Item	Post Ref.	Debit	Credit	Balance	
						Debit	Credit
Apr	30	Adjusting Entry	GJ2	300		300	

Account: Insurance Expense   Account No. 503

Date		Item	Post Ref.	Debit	Credit	Balance	
						Debit	Credit
Apr	30	Adjusting Entry	GJ2	1,000		1,000	

Account: **Rent Expense**   Account No. 504

Date		Item	Post Ref.	Debit	Credit	Balance	
						Debit	Credit
Apr	30	Adjusting Entry	GJ2	1,000		1,000	

Account: **Interest Expense**   Account No. 505

Date		Item	Post Ref	Debit	Credit	Balance	
						Debit	Credit
Apr	30	Adjusting Entry	GJ2	5		5	

6. Prepare an adjusted trial balance.

The adjusted trial balance shows the account balances after the adjusting entries have been recorded in the general journal and posted to the general ledger. Debits and credits on the adjusted trial balance must equal.

Smith Office Supply
Adjusted Trial Balance

For month ended April 30, 2008

Cash	30,000	
Accounts Receivable	4,000	
Prepaid Insurance	11,000	
Prepaid Supplies	200	
Prepaid Rent	11,000	
Inventory	1,000	
Equipment	6,000	
Accumulated Depreciation—Equipment		84
Accounts Payable		11,500
Notes Payable		1,000
Interest Payable		5
John Smith, Capital		50,000
Sales		3,000
Depreciation Expense	84	
Supplies Expense	300	
Insurance Expense	1,000	
Rent Expense	1,000	
Interest Expense	5	
	65,589	65,589

7. Prepare an income statement.

The preparation of the income statement involves revealing the revenue and expenses for the period.

Smith Office Supply
Income Statement

For Month Ended April 30, 2008

Revenue:		
Sales		3,000
Expenses:		
Depreciation Expense	84	
Supplies Expense	300	
Insurance Expense	1,000	
Rent Expense	1,000	
Interest Expense	5	
Total Expenses		2,389
Net Income		611

8. Prepare a retained earnings statement.

The retained earnings statement includes the beginning balance of the retained earnings account, the net income, the dividends paid, and the ending retained earnings balance.

Smith Office Supply
Retained Earnings Statements

For Month Ended April 30, 2008

Retained Earnings, April 1, 2008	0	
Net Income for April	611	
Less: Dividends	0	
Increase in Retained Earnings		611
Retained Earnings, April 30, 2008		611

9. Prepare a balance sheet.

The balance sheet is prepared to show the ending balances in the asset, liability, and equity accounts.

Smith Office Supply
Balance Sheet

30-Apr-08

Current Assets

Cash	30,000	
Accounts Receivable	4,000	
Prepaid Insurance	11,000	
Prepaid Supplies	200	
Prepaid Rent	11,000	
Inventory	1,000	
Total Current Assets		57,200
Property, Plant, and Equipment:		
Equipment	6,000	
Accumulated Depreciation—Equipment	84	
Total Property, Plant, and Equipment		5,916
Total Assets		**63,116**

Liabilities

Current Liabilities:		
Accounts Payable	11,500	
Interest Payable	5	
Total Current Liabilities		11,505
Long-term Liabilities:		
Notes Payable	1,000	
Total Long-term Liabilities		**12,505**

Equity

John Smith, Capital	50,000	
Retained Earnings	611	50,611
Total Liabilities and Equity		**63,116**

10. Prepare closing entries for the month in the general journal.

Closing entries are recorded in the general journal in order to close all temporary revenue and expense accounts.

General Journal

Date		Description	Posting Ref.	Debit	Credit
		Closing Entries			
Apr	30	Sales	401	3,000	
		Income Summary	303		3,000
Apr	30	Income Summary	303	2,389	
		Depreciation Expense	501		84
		Supplies Expense	502		300
		Insurance Expense	503		1,000
		Rent Expense	504		1,000
		Interest Expense	505		5
Apr	30	Income Summary	303	611	
		Retained Earnings	302		611

11. Post closing entries in the general ledger.

Closing entries are transferred from the general journal to the respective accounts in the general ledger.

Account: Cash   **Account No. 101**

Date		Item	Post Ref.	Debit	Credit	Balance Debit	Balance Credit
Apr	1		GJ1	50,000		50,000	
	3		GJ1		12,000	38,000	
	8		GJ1		12,000	26,000	
	9		GJ1	3,000		29,000	
	10		GJ1	1,000		30,000	

Account: Accounts Receivable   **Account No. 102**

Date		Item	Post Ref.	Debit	Credit	Balance Debit	Balance Credit
Apr	5		GJ1	2,000		2,000	
	6		GJ1	2,000		4,000	

Account: Prepaid Insurance   **Account No. 103**

Date		Item	Post Ref.	Debit	Credit	Balance	
						Debit	Credit
Apr	3		GJ1	12,000		12,000	
	30	Adjusting Entry	GJ2		1,000	11,000	

Account: Prepaid Supplies   **Account No. 104**

Date		Item	Post Ref.	Debit	Credit	Balance	
						Debit	Credit
Apr	2		GJ1	500		500	
	30	Adjusting Entry	GJ2		300	200	

Account: Prepaid Rent   **Account No. 105**

Date		Item	Post Ref.	Debit	Credit	Balance	
						Debit	Credit
Apr	8		GJ1	12,000		12,000	
	30	Adjusting Entry	GJ2		1,000	11,000	

Account: Inventory   **Account No. 106**

Date		Item	Post Ref.	Debit	Credit	Balance	
						Debit	Credit
Apr	4		GJ1	5,000		5,000	
	5		GJ1		2,000	3,000	
	6		GJ1		2,000	1,000	

Account: Equipment   **Account No. 107**

Date		Item	Post Ref.	Debit	Credit	Balance	
						Debit	Credit
Apr	7		GJ1	6,000		6,000	

Account: Accumulated Depreciation—Equipment   **Account No. 108**

Date		Item	Post Ref.	Debit	Credit	Balance	
						Debit	Credit
Apr	30	Adjusting Entry	GJ2		84		84

Account: Accounts Payable Account No. 201

Date		Item	Post Ref.	Debit	Credit	Balance Debit	Balance Credit
Apr	2		GJ1		500		500
	4		GJ1		5,000		5,500
	7		GJ1		6,000		11,500

Account: Notes Payable Account No. 202

Date		Item	Post Ref.	Debit	Credit	Balance Debit	Balance Credit
Apr	10		GJ1		1,000		1,000

Account: Interest Payable Account No. 203

Date		Item	Post Ref.	Debit	Credit	Balance Debit	Balance Credit
Apr	30	Adjusting Entry	GJ2		5		5

Account: John Smith, Capital   Account No. 301

Date		Item	Post Ref.	Debit	Credit	Balance Debit	Balance Credit
Apr	1		GJ1		50,000		50,000

Account: Retained Earnings   Account No. 302

Date		Item	Post Ref.	Debit	Credit	Balance Debit	Balance Credit
Apr	30	Closing Entry	GJ3		611		611

Account: Income Summary   Account No. 303

Date		Item	Post Ref.	Debit	Credit	Balance Debit	Balance Credit
Apr	30	Closing Entry	GJ3		3,000		3,000
	30	Closing Entry	GJ3	2,389			611
	30	Closing Entry	GJ3	611			0

Account: Sales   Account No. 401

Date		Item	Post Ref.	Debit	Credit	Balance Debit	Credit
Apr	9		GJ1		3,000		3,000
	30	Closing Entry	GJ3	3,000		0	0

Account: Supplies Expense   Account No. 502

Date		Item	Post Ref.	Debit	Credit	Balance Debit	Credit
Apr	30	Adjusting Entry	GJ2	300		300	
	30	Closing Entry	GJ3		300	0	0

Account: Insurance Expense   Account No. 503

Date		Item	Post Ref.	Debit	Credit	Balance Debit	Credit
Apr	30	Adjusting Entry	GJ2	1,000		1,000	
	30	Closing Entry	GJ3		1,000	0	0

Account: Rent Expense   Account No. 504

Date		Item	Post Ref.	Debit	Credit	Balance Debit	Balance Credit
Apr	30	Adjusting Entry	GJ2	1,000		1,000	
	30	Closing Entry	GJ3		1,000	0	0

Account: Interest Expense   Account No. 505

Date		Item	Post Ref.	Debit	Credit	Balance Debit	Balance Credit
Apr	30	Adjusting Entry	GJ2	5		5	
	30	Closing Entry	GJ3		5	0	0

12. Prepare a post-closing trial balance.

The post-closing trial balance is prepared in order to provide an accurate and up-to-date balance of all permanent accounts including assets, liabilities, and equity accounts.

Smith Office Supply
Post Closing Trial Balance

For Month Ended April 30, 2008

Cash	30,000	
Accounts Receivable	4,000	
Prepaid Insurance	11,000	
Prepaid Supplies	200	
Prepaid Rent	11,000	
Inventory	1,000	
Equipment	6,000	
Accumulated Depreciation—Equipment		84
Accounts Payable		11,500
Notes Payable		1,000
Interest Payable		5
John Smith, Capital		50,000
Retained Earnings		611
	63,200	**63,200**

ABOUT THE AUTHOR

Rita Gritton Mallory has thirty-five years experience in business education teaching accounting at the secondary and post-secondary level. She earned her BA and MS in Business Education with thirty-nine hours above the Masters level from Eastern Kentucky University in Richmond, Kentucky. Her husband is Alan, and she has two children, Sarah and Adam. Rita was influenced to go into the education field by her father who treasured education and told her that "money, power, health, and everything else in life could all be taken away, but no one can ever take away your education and your degree."

Printed in the United States
130214LV00005B/19/P